happinesswise

poems

Jonathan Bennett

ECW

Published by ECW Press
665 Gerrard Street East, Toronto, ON M4M 1Y2
416-694-3348 / info@ecwpress.com

Library and Archives Canada Cataloguing in Publication

Bennett, Jonathan, 1970–, author
Happinesswise : poems / Jonathan Bennett.

Issued in print and electronic formats.
ISBN 978-1-77041-428-0 (softcover); ISBN 978-1-77305-201-4 (PDF); ISBN 978-1-77305-200-7 (epub)

I. Title.

PS8553.E534H37 2018 C811'.6 C2017-906206-9
C2017-906207-7

Editor for the press: Michael Holmes | a misFit book
Author photo: Rebekah Littlejohn
Cover and type: Rachel Ironstone

The publication of *Happinesswise* has been generously supported by the Canada Council for the Arts, which last year invested $153 million to bring the arts to Canadians throughout the country, and by the Government of Canada through the Canada Book Fund. *Nous remercions le Conseil des arts du Canada de son soutien. L'an dernier, le Conseil a investi 153 millions de dollars pour mettre de l'art dans la vie des Canadiennes et des Canadiens de tout le pays. Ce livre est financé en partie par le gouvernement du Canada.* We also acknowledge the support of the Ontario Arts Council (OAC), an agency of the Government of Ontario, which last year funded 1,737 individual artists and 1,095 organizations in 223 communities across Ontario for a total of $52.1 million, and the contribution of the Government of Ontario through the Ontario Book Publishing Tax Credit and the Ontario Media Development Corporation.

Canada Council for the Arts | Conseil des Arts du Canada | Canada

Ontario | Ontario Media Development Corporation

ONTARIO ARTS COUNCIL
CONSEIL DES ARTS DE L'ONTARIO
an Ontario government agency
un organisme du gouvernement de l'Ontario

Printed and bound in Canada
Coach House 5 4 3 2 1

Also by Jonathan Bennett

Poetry

Happinesswise (2018)

Civil and Civic (2011)

Here is my street, this tree I planted (2004)

Fiction

Colonial Hotel (2014)

Entitlement (2008)

Verandah People (2003)

After Battersea Park (2001)

Contents

for Haley

happinesswise

Palliative Care Reflective Portfolio

Patient No. 1

Do I? Admit to the neighbour I need help?
She'll offer impatience, weak Earl Grey.

So instead I admit myself, impatiently,
thrown into that time-worn, off-grey ward

whose Hospitalists chart my chest rattle.
I suffer no fear. I am the recipient

of patient-centred, evidence-based care.
This promise made to me all alone,

on a wipe-able poster that's reinforced
by a tenderly chosen stock photo paired

with a font inspired by Cézanne's cursive.
I curse the machine drone, the urine sting,

the sour C. diff smell, the pump throb,
the infection control, latex-free signage.

Only last March, the lake icy, gin and tonics,
tinkling wind chimes, your still-beautiful clavicle.

I presented to the ER with severe pain
in my lower—well, does it really matter

where this began? Things have evolved.
Let's keep up, I say. But he taps my gut.

Read the chart, I bark. He does, mumbles
left flank. I am deemed incapacitated.

Last summer I was myself. That recently,
really, independent, with plans in place.

I golfed. Was a snow bird. I hear this,
my diminished life as a chart note,

a biography no one considered worthy—
is it ever too late for morbid thoughts?

You dear, are elsewhere, gone in that
peculiar way—off the wall, in a facility

with advanced dementia. At the lake
last summer your dress removed one

afternoon for no reason and we stared
at each other until we remembered

the way it was done, by us. That was the last
time our bodies knew their lines. The first?

Another century. Same lake. We giggled—
poke, poke, poke. The results

of investigations indicate—no, wait for it,
I require a biopsy of the ilium lesion

for a definitive diagnosis, but a working
one: metastatic renal cell carcinoma.

It chisels into me, their grave tones,
but I joke, adding colourful grace notes—

they do not know, I know, the meaning.

Before a doctor dies he becomes a person—
mortality being a prerequisite for death,

which occurs to me in a postscript thought.
My goals: pain relief, symptom control. Not curative.

I do not speak, but am understood by blinking coyly
at said plan. My son has arrived. He is a doctor too.

He has a new wife. Younger, a prototype
of the previous, more luxurious version.

Their language is useless here because
I still understand it, even if I can no longer—

The resident's mind is so fresh it's still setting.
What are the words for that thing I wish to pray?

I try to say to him, and he leans in,
I try to whisper to him: *Overdose me.*

He looks aghast. Did I manage to make a sound?
He says, what I am about to share is going

to be difficult to hear. My son and the resident
are speaking. I am still, listening. The cancer.

Likely metastatic. Left kidney. Multiple locations.

My next steps are to determine I cannot walk.
My son's first steps—across the lichen at the lake.

Radiation might be an option for symptom control.
It is not a cure. They discuss goals for my care.

My son takes the news hard. He is emotional.
He is relying on his child-wife for comfort,

condolence. I use my eyes to indicate Kleenex
without meaning, it has a tone of reprimand.

Comfort is assured. Remembering questions
can be hard. Try to write them down.

Pain and symptom teams get involved
and former colleagues in Radiation

Oncology and Orthopedics are called upon.
Or maybe they are just visitors. They see

themselves in me. Smile. The first week
my agony begins to modestly improve,

I am told. I walk a length of the hospital
ward with much discomfort, I am told.

Options for care outside of the hospital
are discussed, I am told. I cannot return

home. I will not be cared for at my son's
home—for a reason never addressed.

I wish to be reunited with my wife,
but I cannot speak. A social worker

I was routinely rude to intuits what
no one else can and applies for spousal

reunification on compassionate grounds.
I apologize to her all night.

The resident finished his rotation today.
Dictated, in all seriousness, into his small

machine final thoughts for his Palliative Care
Reflective Portfolio:

The patient is optimistic
he might be discharged to his demented wife.

Patient No. 2

Chin stubble, those few stubborn white whiskers
that ignore my news—I am an 87-year-old male

and I must be shaved. It's how I face the day.
The signs mount: Acute. Bed 6. Sharps Disposal.

According to the triage information, he confirms
chest pain after the blood transfusion last week—

My wife shades in the story. The facts remain true.

I am a ten-year-old boy with itchy woollen socks.
A few words of English and castor sugar at my lip.

Toboggan, Christmas, tinsel, fruit, Ontario.
It is '36. I've come from Bonn to undreamed cold.

My emersion begins the day I alight the *Bremen*
in New York. I ask my mother for a new name.

My German is abandoned. My accent becomes
an enemy I scrub at until all my words are clean.

While there were no changes on his EKG
it's apparent that he's sustained an MI based

on the rise in troponin, what this means . . .
What this means, she explains for me, is that I want

just comfort. No heroics, she says heroically.
We'd agreed 87 is a fine age to let the past pass.

I am still in here. A doctor reintroduces himself.
He is surprised that, with only my eyes, I seem

to recognize him, that my wife remembers his name.

They discuss my care goals, and she says I know
that my heart is a weakling. *It's from the severe*

aortic stenosis and the recent NSTEMI.
I am making slow progress. I could fail

at any time. She is finding it emotionally hard,
she says to him, to leave me alone in the hospital.

It's empty at home. She looks tired but not old.
She becomes tearful. Can I return home with her?

Please. Doctor, what is the worst that could happen?
Might not be a good plan given his frailty and fall risk.

He says that she will make it through all this.

She has pinned up a life-sized poster of the German
soccer player I admire on my hospital room wall.

I missed the final. But my wife has recorded the game.
We will watch it together, she says, when you come.

He continues to progress and is walking with less difficulty.
A plan is hatched to return me home—to our small

apartment with nursing support. Everyone is happy.

I fall. Admitted again. I cannot catch my breath.
Somehow, I survived that first evening, my wife explains

to a new nurse, against great odds. No, not a nurse.
She is a doctor. She smiles, skipping over our mistake,

and says maybe this is just where he was meant to be.

I visit Bonn upon retirement, walk the streets in corduroys
and kneel in a cathedral. I do not pray so much as apologize

to my dead mother, whose funeral I missed out of anger
years ago. Later I drink a tall, thin glass of pilsner

and read a novel in the sunshine and see young people
talk on phones and laugh. This was all some years ago.

Now only my wife is at my bedside. She strokes
my face, says that she will shave me tomorrow.

I am thankful, but I have forgotten her name again.
She is telling me about the soccer match we watched

together. The near-miss penalty, the tied final score.

Patient No. 3

Why now? When the game is in its dying seconds,
a final time out—the inevitable drawn out—the doc lays

his papers and cell phone on the sheet next to me,
the bedside television, mega bucks, a subscription

that is all profit—it's called a *day-to-day plan.*

I asked who was winning, he said.

This doc's fading British accent is cheery.
His people were once from India.

I asked you, why do you think you are in hospital.
I asked you, if you were in any pain or discomfort.
I asked you, if I might examine you. I'm repeating

myself, he said, because I require consent. Referee
calls the game. Dejection, elation, kissing cousins.

I am a skeleton of my former self, I say. He speaks!
Your muscles have wasted and here, your abdomen's

bloated with ascetic fluid. Eyes sunken but, look,
I can see a twinkle. There's that mischievous smile.

They all come now. The television is flicked off.
Talking starts all around me, my nameless body,

I am a sack of shit, I think. This is a teachable moment,
I learn. The patient's record ballooned after a prolonged

stay in the ICU and step down, says the British doctor.
Shortly after examining the patient, I met with his two

sons who inquired about his current functional status
and prognosis which was, even days ago, quite poor.

I am Phil. I am a retired truck driver. Thirty-seven years.
On the way back, I'm up north hauling toothpicks,

I phone but no answer. Turns out the wife's gone.
Took no money but left the dogs. Take them one last

time to go pot a Bambi. They run coon instead.
Can't drive and keep dogs very well, can I?

So, I released them down in the city—in that nice part
with double garages and trampolines—so some rich

prick will take them in all right. Get them fat.
Otherwise they'd have to take a brick-and-bag dip.

The patient had been living independently in his own home
prior to admission to the hospital. The sons seemed either

unaware or ill-informed about the poor prognosis. So?
Inform the patient and his family of his terminal

illness and change the patient's code status to a DNR.
Why? Based on the perceived hopelessness of resuscitative

efforts for a man without a functioning liver. Correct.

So? Assess the patient's competence to make an informed
decision about his advanced directives and determine

the appointed substitute decision maker. All agree? Good.

When I first met the patient, I felt that he was competent
to make his own decisions but seemed to poorly grasp

his diagnosis and prognosis. Or be in some form of denial?
Does this look like a psych rotation? I explained to his sons

that I would be surprised if he survived this admission.
He is competent now, but this will not continue, I said.

Did they understand? Yes, they saw he was sick, but no,
my concerns about hepatic encephalopathy were lost on them.

One son held on to hope of recovery and another wondered
if transplant might be an option. Then the patient's clinical

status deteriorated precipitously. He had the ascetic fluid
drained multiple times by paracentesis. Developed infection,

he was hypotensive but any fluid he was given
seemed to immediately accumulate in his abdomen

worsening his precarious cardio-respiratory status.
He was also in renal failure and diuretics were not working.

The family insisted on continuing IV fluids and NG Jevity
feeds which seemed to only worsen his electrolyte status.

I was frank with the family, that I fully expected the patient
to die on multiple occasions (and yet he continued to battle on).

Family began to understand the futility of the situation
and agreed to a DNR and involved the pain and symptom

service to arrange for a transfer to the Palliative ward.

He comes and goes? Family are unwilling to stop feeding
and fluids. His IV was reduced to TKVO and we broached

discontinuing the NG feeds and repeated blood work.

My son is putting a sucker on my tongue. No. It's just
a blue sponge with water on it, keeping my mouth moist.

In high school I restored a '57 Chevy. We parked at the end
of a gravel road, on a rock overlooking a fast river, where

in the summer I went fishing with my father. The smell
of leaf rot and grease, in the back seat she rolled onto

me and we humped and whooped. She must have forgot
that night. Marriage to a long-haul trucker will do that.

The herniated disk, bottles of Jack, unfinished deck.
There's that mischievous smile and twinkle in your eyes.

Be comforted to know your father's suffering has ceased. Healing isn't just about the patient. We all need to be truly

present for loved ones at the end of life. It's a gift to be here.

Concession Lines Signs

Unassumed Road

That day we lost the hound down the way,
watched it bound tongue-slack, freedom-struck
beyond the yellow wood and lichen-crusted
boulders of pink shield rock and undergrowth.
That day we took chances, pressed on.
That day made no difference, even as you
plunged into a field of bemused heifers,
cursing all dogs, as it rolled in steaming dung.

That day we bushwhacked calling its name,
calling it names, until it returned
with a meaty bone that looked like a rib.
A last laugh that day, when glibly
you said, the person who nailed the sign
This Road is Unassumed has trust issues.

Vegetarians Use the Back Door

The cedar smoke and truck exhaust
of a ribfest at hot noon and white
Canadian men lick fingers
and use lite beer as mouthwash,
cupping the rolls of themselves—
or the wife—giving the flesh
a bit of a jiggle, having a good laugh.

Pre-diabetic with gorgeous tits, this one
guy talks so loud not even Stevie Nicks
from the Jimmy six down drowns him out.
Prolly won't run coon. Might run bear?
Then he shoots you a look. *Yes you,*
broccoli boy. Come party with us then.
Just how were you holding your face?

Traffic Calming Ahead

I see the laser eye, like a bindi
between descending digits each
an eyelid batting numbers until
I back off to rickshaw speed,
enter a village that will not long
accept an Oriental trope.

Nothing here is foreign.
Everything belongs.

Yes, but the couple who own
the general store are Goan,
originally, and there's a roadside
rib shack, real Louisiana bark
to tempt bass fishing southerners,
or hungry Yankees up after deer.

I see a harvest moon,
like a Harley's headlight.

It crests a pitching Otonabee hill,
makes a cow a ghost in a field.
The moon a smudge that comes, goes
behind clouds, between firs,
shafts of light climb the ridgeline
until it turns away. Then nothing.

I enter the village late.
Later than anyone else?

Signs for butter tarts and bait
glide by until the exiting traffic
from the arena parking lot halts
progress. A wedding dress and tux
teeter in the back of a Ford F250.
The truck nuts swing. Locals cheer.

Fresh Cut Fries

A hairpin turn dragged the escarpment's
serrated edge, scoring sky. A chip truck.
You and I argued road sign grammar.
(I bemoaned the lost art of the adverb,
you advanced the hyphen, either way.)

Shield rock nursed pockets of April snow
in its nooks of dark. We were so remote.
We ate at a picnic table, by a lake
that we could agree was not *lead* grey.

Your salty mouth now unlocked, eager
to lick me clean. So, jump-cut to me
in a middle-distance, dappled remove.
My point of view is a weak shaky-cam,
as even the ending was wrested away.

Free Metal Drop Off

Solar farm bling blinds both sets of eyes,
surprises me and the well-fed coyote
who then lopes after three wild
turkeys in a field of clover. It's sunrise.

The woman ahead pulls a U-turn, filming
the chase scene on her phone, pointing
with her other hand. Look. There. *There.*

Her friend shimmies out the driver's side.
She bends over the hood, stretches out,
yawns, her posture betraying a bit of yoga,
soreness soothed by the engine's warmth.

Two shots are fired by a guy in a pickup.
Buddy walks into the field, gun broken
over an arm, collects a turkey by its neck.

The remaining birds bicker but hightail it
for a ravine. The dog needles a taut weave
among solar panels and the girl still films
but now pouts for a photo at arm's length,

for when she stitches it together tonight,
adds in a tune she's been killing lately,
the one with snare, that guy from Montreal.

I heave galvanized pipe. Its weight cracks
down into the Dumpster, somehow louder
than the earlier shots, and everyone—
the girl, her friend, the coyote, buddy,

even the two turkeys—all halt abruptly.
Look rudely at me. What? I thought
this was all over. I felt I was good to go.

Third Concession Line

Dawn glint lights up slug-slick on a fly screen.
Theirs is all journey. Beyond those coloured
fractals are flight paths of grackles busy
persecuting a crow above the ditch and berm
in a dogfight over control of air space.

Gaps between drywall and joists are ignored
unless asbestos piping spawns worry.
Such plumbing (well water to showerhead)
is best left be, or particulate will
nest in the welcome wetness of young lungs.

High above the third concession line,
warm air yields to cold and a rotating wall
cloud organizes with no real aim, just journey.
Like an old wives' tale cows lie down in wait.

Neurotypical Sketches

Now We Are Six and Sure

That's impossible, that's impossible—
and it would seem so to me, as a father knows only
what he was taught, primarily, in primary school,
a time when facts were handed down by authorized
authority, except, of course, everything has been corrected.

Do you know what, do you know what—
they've re-frocked Pluto after all, periodically added spurious
new elements that fizz in a second, reset the Mayan glyphs in stone,
and now, astonishingly, the genome informs on your forefather
who enjoyed a bit of Neanderthal on the side.

I know what's common; I know what's rare—
all this fluid evidence equals hurricane status for a six-year-old
finally diagnosed, stoned on a Nova marathon. I'm with him.
Does a peat-preserved man really need an MRI? So how about some
certainty for a change? Make up your goddamned minds.

They Will Take My Island

For days, he digs a hole in the garden deep
enough to climb in, which he does now,
the tightness of it about right for a boy of ten,
the top of his head poking out of the mulch.
He is larval. At one with his beloved insects,
murmuring, worrying about F3 tornadoes.

I reach in, the earth ripe and alive, to calm
him with my weight. He is melting down,
trying to return to the earth, where bacteria
is simple and there are clear rules outlining
how organisms act. My breathy words aimed
at his neck. Tears. Cut roots. Midge. Fecundity.

At night, it's fear of the deep that sweeps across
the bow of his sleep. He is wedged against me,
a father as ballast or, I give up, maybe keel,
until daylight erases his dark horrors measured
in fathoms, or leagues, broken only by facts like
the healing bioluminescence of an angler fish.

Lately, my chief complaint is with language.
I pin one thing to another when a subject
resists simplicity. Mystifying not clarifying.
So, we resort to basic weights, measures,
units of touch, shares of love, to form meaning.
But there are more holes. There are other oceans.

His Charge

I race a light brigade of taxis advancing
to the beat of the change in lights down

King Street. Relax. He is found. Jammed
into the folds of a Moreton Bay Fig

naming the parts of an ant—head, trunk,
metasoma. He's wilted, ducking Sydney's

exhaust, from the need to read all chalked
menus aloud in full, sour cherry bread with

poached rhubarb ricotta and orange jelly.
Exoskeleton. Not covered by skin

and muscles and tissue like humans.
You are a human. Ant eyes are a lot

like fly eyes, connected eyes, seared
barramundi with baby leeks, an ant's

head has two pinchers, to carry food, fight.
Baked goat's cheese soufflé, baby beetroot.

Ants store food in a pocket in their mouth.
Did you know that ants have a poison sack?

Honeycomb. Ants are closely related to wasps.
No blood vessels. Passion fruit. No lungs.

The heart is a long tube. Toasted Almonds.
The nervous system is a long cord that forks,

like a human spine. Figs. Ants. You. Mine.

Sunrise with Sea Monsters

Where there is doubt, there is
information stacked upon data
shoved in between factoids
that I catch and lob back.

If you could just open your mind, he says,
you could begin to believe the evidence.

Air brakes expel, he ducks
as if shot at, flaps, we normalize
the autistic moment for passersby
who flip us stares of weird or pity.

If you could believe the evidence, he says,
eventually your mind would begin to open.

Where is radical cool? Frequently
missed across the dial, surely.
I catch and lob back white noise
at his tween mind, squelching, sonic rubble.

arctic
uncharted
wanderland
kendak strait
boreal forest
factory district
floralis
Rep of terrerius
New Pangea
giga desert
thofs prison
path to Riches
the ruins
inland ocean
Redland
great city
zentis
crimeson beaches
curse of black water
thornti
aust
kratzia
arctic

In Relief

Lately, he says *lemon squares* a lot
and at night with his service dog

hard pressed to him, he admits worries:
I don't know what I'm supposed to do.

Where am I supposed to be right now?
Sleep wind. His oscillating fan is Larry.

There is an entire imaginary world
that he develops alongside this one.

It's a logical realm that makes sense,
a refuge from fluorescent bulb flicker

and persistent AdeleMaroon5Bieber
folded into every wrinkle of existence.

He asks: *Do cyclops blink or wink?*
We laugh and I ask him to tell me

the riddle of Theseus's ship again
because I can't get enough of him

charting his way through a paradox.
And to hear him argue the case

for Bigfoot is to doubt everything
you thought was true in the universe.

Not a day goes by that I don't ask
what the word he just used means.

Lately, he says *lemon squares* a lot.
I know why he adores Coltrane and Dalí.

Somewhere in his new world a city
is being mapped and named and whole

boroughs intricately sketched,
creatures are homed, or else they war.

All this while he thinks of a video game,
turns over some science he's trying

to solve, and four or five other, unrelated
items in a simultaneous, asynchronous

moment that we partly share, he and I
laughing at the bat of a cyclopean eye.

On Occasion

Notes After Fort Worth

It's a lethal dose margarita, freeze, salt, shiver then slap
that sends us back, no fair crack, to swapping sloppy crap
from Southern Cross boyhoods, night cricket, girls and that.

Footnoting *Picnic at Hanging Rock*, me humming
"US Forces," we walk about the old stockyards, here
but not here (you Ballarat, me Cronulla) before we list

at Remington's *The Luckless Hunter*, we recognize
that pale-faced Apache as yet another last Aborigine,
one sentenced to brave it alone through ancestral lands,

every lone star a tombstone, every sound a lost noun,
every remorseful painting an additional subtraction.
This is for the tourists. This is not for the tourists at all.

We stall before a vainglorious statue of a cowboy
wrangling a writhing bull: Man triumphs over bronze.
Then heel-and-toe it over Western heroes, star-stamped

into the trail, set to favourably brand history, or its opposite,
as a family films two dudes on horses, neon winks: *Sirloin!*
As oil-sprung Caravaggios fill museums, contrasting light and crude.

Notes After Glasgow

i.

Plummeting impromptu toward Saltcoats, when a funnel cloud organized,
as the kids went symphonic in the back,
as an audience—a flock of Scottish Blackface—agreed,
as the ancient piled fences upgraded to runway markers,
as we all got out right underneath the thing,
as hail was followed by stony silence, then hail,
as the sky reopened for business with an inky apology
it spun us onward toward the Firth of Clyde for Irn-Bru, or coffee, or tea.

ii.

A tour guide piped on about the Red Douglases, the Earl of Angus,
as if one might materialize on the curtain wall
just now and slaughter us with his stink,
as thousands of gannets and we—
soared across the Firth of Forth to Bass Rock—
as we did when "the War of Rough Wooing bypassed
Tantallon due to the Earl's English sympathies."
The kids whispered turret, dungeon and caught moths at this, the other sea.

iii.

We sang it like a gauche of sightseers on the banks of Loch Lomond,
as we collected up smooth blue and white glass
as if pieces, shapes, colours of our Scots genes,
as a cud-chewing highland cow loitered nearby in heather,
as a gauzy grey sky bled yellow light
on a single dory working headstrong into the chop,
as pant legs were rolled up, the shoreline dancing begun
before rain hemmed us in. Before, we never met again. *No, child, not a sea.*

iv.

A Glasgow without shipyards was hard to swallow for a first-time visitor,
as was the deep-fried frozen pizza served face down on chips,
as we drank in a pub that was once a church—
a wee stumbling congregation of thoughtful souls—
as we solved our problems with vacation-enriched immunity,
as we wandered the halls of the university for sobriety,
as we ambled, finally, through Kelvingrove Museum
and stared down stuffed artefacts and bric-a-brac of the once-known world.

On the Occasion of Her Swearing In

As the young, Indo-Canadian man relieved himself
of tried-and-true, tour-guide gags down the hallways
of the House of Commons, I understood I would cry.

This is why I downed the Chateau Lakeshore.
Why I scarfed the hunk of Senate-cold brie.
Bring them on hot before the day is out. Let me bawl.

Left last in the Library, I called out for my wife
a little too loudly, calling to mind Vermeersch's
impression of Al Purdy pleading for Eurithe.

This is likely why later, I recited "Say the Names"
beneath my breath as we staged brassy irony,
Monsef foreground, Fathers of Confederation

out-of-focus, overhead, tsk-tsking in Victorian—
a soul you mislaid and found again rejoicing.
Cry me Commonwealth tears, *the whole sky falling.*

Yes, this would all be too much. (If you must know,
it came while praying, holding Chief Knott's hand,
in a circle of beliefs—*miigwetch* and *tashakor.*)

Audley Elegy

We are nine strong, meandering the weir
at Audley, talking lazily in twos and threes,

threads gathered, observing foam break,
fold, drift, dissolve. There are currawongs

in the ghost gums, galahs in the kurrajongs
and Ivy skips off counting fairies with Nanny.

Stepped off the verandah, says Auntie Coralie,
wanderer butterflies filled the whole sky—

with orange and black, flying west in swells.
Where do they go? Someone must know.

I am nine, strong, running along the weir
at Audley, the aunts and uncles semicircle,

snags and beer, cricket on the transistor,
bush hot, alive. Soldier ant. Politics.

We are nine strong, meandering the weir
at Audley, a tartan blanket, sandwiches,

pieces of slice. We wait for the southerly.
When will it come? Someone must know.

Let Me Speak Softly of Two Days

Let me speak softly of two days
one in the cold where you teased me
in your British-not-British way
about the Barbour jacket I wore,
how uselessly thin it was against snow.
What's with you Australians anyway
citing class and colonialism but really
not having to say much of anything at all.

The other at Michelle's on Stoney Lake
where the wind and cedars and granite
loosened up your tongue and out came
an escape-from-Burma drama as frightening
and funny as a film except it was your life.
Now, you are with your father having left
pieces of your Ogoni self everywhere
as you went about carrying him with you.

Analogue Analogies

Loggerheads

i.

She writes with a modest burst of thumb quiver—
the sound of a fetal heartbeat has never failed

to make me cry—her eyes drawn away from
the midwife to her phone to share the idea

of these pulsing shadows with her social feed.

ii.

A loggerhead turtle follows her primeval byways,
criss-crossing shipping lanes, garbage floes, long lines

and drift nets, to the sand womb of her own birth,
her own statistically grim beat down the beach,

to the foreshore, undertow, *Sargassum*, long nights
afloat with jellies and the heavens blinking

with global positioning satellites as she eases one
flipper in front of the other, willing herself along.

iii.

She is needed again and again and so must arrive.
She records and exists concurrently, in a pocket

of *just before*, of *right now* and of *very soon*,
she texts while shitting (maybl8), tweets on all fours

beneath him (#àlaprochaine), she feels that her body
is a trap, that her highest plane of existence ought

to hold nothing sacred and should forgo privacy,
living instead inside the secure connection

of the many online threads of her nature.
These are her arteries; she is all circuitry.

She would migrate properly to this existence,
leave her body for dead, except for the baby's idle.

iv.

She dreams she is a turtle, heavy sand on her
flippers, at her throat and mouth as she struggles

toward the water, leaving them there in the hole
to fend for themselves. She knows how it will end

for most. Her heart aches for each one snatched
by a seagull, snake, fish, or curious boy

with a flashlight, chocolate bar, and firecrackers.
In her dream, she swims away leaving them to face

chance as she rolls over in sheets,
in rough surf, undercurrent pulling her away

until above her, night extends its lust
in overwhelming volume and capacity and illness

that wrecks her on an island, beached until dawn
comes calm and confidential like the inside of a shell,

its pink opalescence and soft fleshy tubes, now
turned into silk to suck on having been ripped,

smashed apart, with jaws eager and ancient
that shell, translucence transgressed, busted.

The sea is an ultrasound of murmur,
dissipates and is stillness, stars and a moon.

She writes it all down longhand, the letter shapes
flowing out of the pen from childhood memory alone.

She is anxious to get it right, to save its sad energy
until morning, and in case the turtle means something—

a call from within, a reservation or cancellation—
simple dreams to set her off wet, and briny, with unease.

Manual

They cannot make sense of it all time and again,
so they create a manual to service their needs.

There is a system of sorts at play here,
that divides the information by group sequentially.

"The damn manual's a crutch on which we can no longer rely!"
So they fashion radical theories, letting the manual grow stale.

There is a process of sorts in use here,
that groups the divided information periodically.

They cannot lie to others if they will not to themselves,
so they scapegoat the manual, then redact for an eternity.

There is a procedure of sorts at work here,
that informs the groups by division intuitively.

Finally, they cannot keep straight faces when asked to explain,
so they tell it like it is, citing the manual verbatim without knowing.

Reasonable Assurance

The grey area is immaterial by some measures.
The congested honks of geese rise as they single-file
it across the bitumen into the culvert's grey water.

As I was saying, the grey area is subjective insofar
as there are no bright lines. Look instead to the
reasonable person test or business judgment rule.

Materiality is the auditor's clean opinion: What *is* good
for the gander? Isn't it the nature of geese to seek water,
and don't we forgive goslings because they are vulnerable?

Just decide who is right and who is wrong already.
The longer grey area is navigated, the inkier it appears.
Certainty is nice, but it's never a surety, because, well,

take the marten (not to be confused with the fisher) stalking
the gaggle for hours before exercising its duty of loyalty.
Its ethical model: Gizzards and warm organs are food.

Comply or Explain

You might be anywhere this could be serious.
Christmas anthems and glass and marble fake
an echo of time and colours up and down
escalators galore and the tinsel town—
a serious bitch display—trades at discount
and opens conveniently late so there's
happiness and your people can memory-make
without presence-of-mind or miscount.

You might be here escalating a serious
shop-through instead of taking the piss.
This could be serious if open-late
capitalism isn't euphemism
or enthusiasm. A set of pierced lips claim
this will have teeth so comply or explain.

Swallow the Toad of Disgust

When it is yours—
have "a moment," open up your sash, recant, blame,
keel over laughing, praise it, vomit you cared that much.

When it is his, or hers—
offer sympathy, do an intervention, help, hurt,
cross a leg over, kiss it, aspirin you drank so much.

When it is theirs—
provide context, annotate the system, know, nod,
kneel in solidarity, share it, dry heave the circumference.

When it is ours—
clutch a handful, cry *why* in the streets, bellow, fume,
keen the night away, elegize it, breathe until it's passed.

When it is mine—
realize that I overslept, overate, saw "game over" winking,
know it's about time I collected my hat, handed over the keys.

After St. Ignatius

See everything
a piano is dynamics and
a crowd is organics and
a sauce is harmonics and
a crush teases and frolics.

Turn a blind eye to much
in the dark don't we guess
at how much to redress—
it's blind man's bluff—
hope and grope and luck.

Correct a little
when the wind is favourable
and the players are in time
and the sous chef is loyal
and no one is watching.

Lorenzetti's Allegory of Bad Government

Dairy Queen on Queen Street,
summer and white plump dollops,
ass cracks, served soft atop
a fiery decaled warm hood.

Man, is he cocksure and killer.
She is high with a delicate overbite.
All those short words that may
not be written politely, apply.

To think he'll be a four-term mayor
and she'll have identical twin girls,
go back to school so as to pass
for intelligent in passable company.

At night when they spoon one another
and when she reaches for his stick shift
he'll think of work, press conferences,
committees of the whole, bylaw holes,

and the girl she once was, because,
well, because, together, in a swirl of
cold sugary luck, it reinforces the merit of
secrets well-kept, with a good bonus package.

Happinesswise

An analogue of wonder, this Edison phonograph
at almost one hundred it plays like new
like it always has
                                        in the springtime I throw open
the sash windows, creak on the verandah's swing,
let a foxtrot roam the garden, as it might once have.

Through trial and error, I learn that if you crank
the handle twenty times a record will spin
right the way through:
                                                the sound of it pairing
clarinet and banjo, lovers plucked and blown,
with Mac and Spy blossoms on the apple trees.

Emerging foliage begins to obstruct my lake view.
Soon fat summer leaves and shade will wash it away
with dark and green.
                                                What if I could fell those trees
that crest the ridge? Year-round sightlines of double
blue, water and sky. But they belong to another guy.

Out of the glare, flinch and squint, a floating man
fishing in his aluminum canoe, who surely cannot
see me, up high, concealed.
                                                            Would he mind
that I've been watching him as I sit here listening
to woodwind notes made by breaths drawn long ago?

I believe I know what he's up to in his camouflage cap.
Why he's alone. I'm watching him closely. If he's after
bass he's too early,
                                            pre-season fishing a petty crime,
committed by the impatient. So, is that a shallow cast?
Or just lazy strokes, the thumbing of a paperback novel?

A man escaping the city's news feed, stealing nothing
more than what was already his? A few private hours.
If so, a fortunate man, happinesswise.
                                        I should set
the record straight. With binoculars I could know for sure,
but the song ends, diminuendo into centurial crackle.

Unexpectedly, the floating man (too old to know or care)
hollers out recalcitrant, antiquated wisecracks:
Mind your own business.
                                Oh, poor floating soul,
thinking that nosiness still means something.
Take a picture, it lasts longer. Hey, good one.

Did I mention I'm drinking Oolong? Man becomes
lost in tea and leaves, paddling through reeds
from the lake proper,
                            into the river mouth,
bulrushes, taking his crime, or legal pleasures
with him upstream into gentle embankments.

I have now cranked all the foxtrots. The tea is cold.
The man returns to pastureland. Then must portage
to his car, strap it
                        to the roof and slope homeward.
This is what happens as the lake disappears
due to the onset of summer and the difficulty of trees.

Notes and Acknowledgments

"Palliative Care Reflective Portfolio" is for Dr. Paul Jones (who bravely provided me with his redacted journal that became the jumping off point). The "Patient One" section first appeared in *The Puritan.* It also was included in *The Best Canadian Poetry in English, 2015* (Tightrope Books). Thanks to the editors, especially Jacob McArthur Mooney.

"Neurotypical Sketches" is for my son Thomas Morgan. He has read, edited, and given me his permission to publish these poems. The illustration is a detailed map of Thomas's multi-year, world-building project. It continues to evolve. "They Will Take My Island" and "Sunrise with Sea Monsters" were written for Paul Vermeersch's online projects of the same names. Thanks, Paul.

"Notes After Fort Worth" is for Nathaniel O'Reilly and it first appeared in *Cordite Poetry Review* (Australia).

"Notes After Glasgow" is for Paul Timpson and Haley Bennett.

"On the Occasion of Her Swearing In" is for Maryam Monsef.

"Audley Elegy" is in memory of Coralie McLennan (1944–2015).

"Let Me Speak Softly of Two Days" is in memory of Ken Wiwa (1967–2016).

An earlier version of "Fresh Cut Fries" first appeared in *Prosopisia* (India).

"Manual" was written for the online project *the litter i see.*

•

I acknowledge and am grateful for the financial support over the years of the Ontario Arts Council and the Canada Council for the Arts.

My deepest thanks to Michael Holmes and the good people at ECW. I'm grateful for Emily Schultz whose editorial eye and ear I trust so much. Also, thanks to Adam Sol, Laura Gaughan, and Shelley Hermer who read some of these along the way. Finally, to Wendy, and Thomas and Ivy—all my love.